FULL-SPEED SPORTS

THE SCIENCE OF A FASTBALL

350

TAMRA B. ORR

CHERRY LAKE

Publishing

Published in the United States of America by Cherry Lake Publishing
Ann Arbor, Michigan
www.cherrylakepublishing.com

Content Adviser: David Beaton, youth baseball coach and pitching instructor
Reading Adviser: Marla Conn, ReadAbility, Inc.

Photo Credits: © bmcent1/iStock.com, cover, 1, 26; © Aspen Photo/Shutterstock.com, 5, 10, 13; © Jamie Roach/
Shutterstock.com, 6; © Everett Historical/Shutterstock Images, 9; © John Kershner/Shutterstock.com, 14;
© jpbcpa/iStock.com, 15; © Toddtaulman | Dreamstime.com - Aroldis Chapman Photo, 16; © Skyhawk x/Shutterstock
Images, 19; © St Petersburg Times/ZUMAPRESS/Newscom, 20; ©Highwaystarz-Photography, 21 ; © Photo Works/
Shutterstock.com, 22; © MICHAEL S. WIRTZ/MCT/Newscom, 25; © Americanspirit | Dreamstime.com - Dodger Fans
Photo, 28

Library of Congress Cataloging-in-Publication Data

Orr, Tamra.
  The science of a fastball/Tamra B. Orr.
    pages cm.—(Full-Speed Sports)
  Includes index.
  Audience: Age: 8–12.
  Audience: Grade: 4 to 6.
  ISBN 978-1-63362-582-2 (hardcover)—ISBN 978-1-63362-762-8 (pdf)—ISBN 978-1-63362-672-0 (paperback)—
ISBN 978-1-63362-852-6 (ebook)
  1. Pitching (Baseball)—Juvenile literature. I. Title.

  GV871.O77 2015
  796.357'22—dc23

                        2014049844

Cherry Lake Publishing would like to acknowledge the work of
the Partnership for 21st Century Skills. Please visit www.p21.org
for more information.

Printed in the United States of America
Corporate Graphics

ABOUT THE AUTHOR

Tamra Orr is the author of more than 400 books for readers of all ages. Tamra, who has four grown
kids, lives in the Pacific Northwest with her husband, dog, and cat. She is a graduate of Ball State
University and spends most of her free time reading, camping, and finding out more about the
world around her.

TABLE OF CONTENTS

CHAPTER 1

LET'S PLAY BALL!

All eyes are on the **pitcher**. He pauses a moment to watch for what type of pitch the **catcher** will signal. Will it be a curveball, knuckleball, slider, or fastball? The catcher signals, and the pitcher nods. Slowly, the right-hander lifts his left leg and faces third base. The crowd holds its breath. A fastball it is.

As his left foot touches the ground, the pitcher rotates his chest, shoulders, and **pelvis** toward home plate. Finally, he releases the baseball in a whipping motion. His palm faces the batter, and his fingers give an extra push to the ball. It moves in a blur! The batter swings and misses.

The power in a fastball is astounding! The ball often hits speeds of 90 miles (145 kilometers) per hour—or more. Experts have determined that pitching a fastball puts the same amount of stress on the arm as if the

A right-handed pitcher lifts up his left leg before striding toward the plate.

pitcher had thrown a 60-pound (27 kilograms) weight. The shoulder has to rotate faster than any movement of the body in any other sport.

For most young players, playing baseball is about having fun—running for home, trying not to strike out, and throwing a pitch to challenge the batter. For professional players, baseball is much more than a

*Every player on the team has an important job,
but none is more important than the pitcher.*

game. It is their job—and they are often rewarded for winning games or championships.

Every player on a baseball team has an important job, but perhaps the most important job is the pitcher. The execution of flawless pitches that will stump each batter are often key to determining the game's winner. The pitcher who throws a fastball has to be strong, determined, and skillful. The fastball is—as its name states—very, very fast. And it is very hard on the pitcher's body.

GO DEEPER!

Typically, the speed of a fastball is measured by using a radar gun. This gun is held in the hand and is often used by police officers to check if cars are exceeding the speed limit on the highways. What other sports might use a radar gun, and what might they measure?

FROM AMATEUR TO MAJOR LEAGUE

Can you imagine Union soldiers playing baseball while in Confederate prisoner-of-war camps during the Civil War? They did, which shows how long baseball has been part of American culture. No one is sure exactly when the game was invented, but by the mid-1800s, it had already established rules and competitions. By 1860, baseball had become the most popular game in the United States.

At first, **amateurs** made up the teams, meaning everyone played for fun and not for money. That changed when the first professional baseball team formed in 1869:

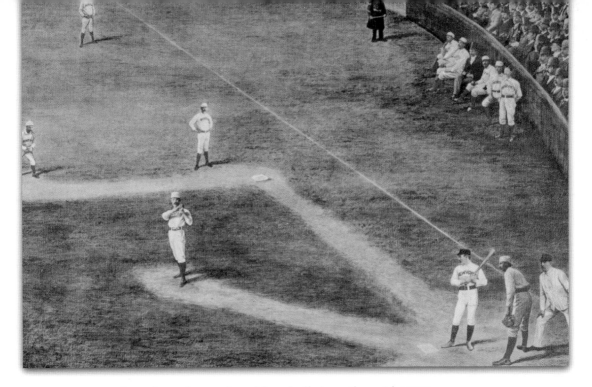

Americans have played baseball since the mid-1800s.

the Cincinnati Red Stockings. The team paid their players to play baseball. More and more teams formed, and soon major league baseball was thriving. People of all ages followed the games, rooting for their favorites to win.

In the beginning of baseball history, throwing the ball hard and fast was not allowed. The game was supposed to be about running from base to base, catching balls, and hitting home runs. Fans and players alike frowned upon a pitcher who threw the ball too hard. Despite this,

This batter has swung too late and missed the fastball.

[21ST CENTURY SKILLS LIBRARY]

pitchers began perfecting their methods to throw a ball so fast that a batter hardly had time to respond. The crowds loved the fastball. They wanted to see more of it!

As fastballs became common, the National League had to move the pitching mound back more than 10 feet (3 meters) so there was more space between the pitcher and the batter. It has remained at 60 feet, 6 inches (18.5 m) ever since.

Today, fastballs are still the most popular pitches among pitchers and fans. But if you happen to be the batter, you just hope you can move fast enough to hear the crack of the bat against the ball—and not the sound of the umpire saying "Stri-i-i-i-i-ke!"

THINK ABOUT IT!

A baseball racing through the air at 100 miles (161 km) per hour (mph) may not sound that fast, but think about it. That is almost twice the legal speed limit when driving on the highway. Winds moving at 100 mph would knock you down and qualify as an F-1 tornado. What else can you think of that goes 100 mph?

CHAPTER 3

THE FINE ART OF A FASTBALL

Whiz! When a fastball speeds by at 90 or 100 miles (145 or 161 km) per hour, it can be difficult to tell what kind of fastball it is. Pitchers throw a variety of fastballs. The difference lies in how the pitcher grips and throws the ball.

The most common types of fastballs are *four-seam, two-seam, cut,* and *split-finger.* Each one depends on where the pitcher places his middle and index fingers and thumb and how he releases the ball. The key to a fastball is aiming directly at the plate and allowing the ball to roll off the fingers as they snap down. This puts a backspin on the ball.

Most pitchers can throw multiple types of fastballs.

As a fastball spins through the air, it creates an envelope of air around it. This is known as a **boundary layer**. As it spins, a difference in air pressure is created between the top and bottom of the ball. This air pressure, plus the position of the ball's stitches, can cause the ball to "drag" and change its direction. This is referred to as the Magnus effect.

Throwing a fastball is about more than a spinning ball, some air currents, and **aerodynamics**, however. None of that matters without a baseball pitcher who has spent hours

Roy Oswalt, from the Houston Astros, warms up before a spring training game in 2010.

14

A radar gun can measure pitches' speeds.

and hours practicing, as well as training his body to take on the demands of throwing a ball fast and hard.

A number of pitchers have fired 90 mph (145 kph) fastballs, but throwing a ball that reaches 100 mph (161 kph) or faster is quite a skill. Many baseball **statisticians** keep records on who has been able to do this so far in history. One of the earliest was a 107.6 mph (173.1 kph) fastball thrown by Bob Feller in 1946.

In the past decade, the number of pitchers hitting triple-digit speeds has soared. So far, no one has beat

Cuban pitcher Aroldis Chapman, from the Cincinnati Reds, has come close to breaking the record for fastest pitch.

[21ST CENTURY SKILLS LIBRARY]

Nolan Ryan's record of 108.1 mph (173.9 kph) in 1974, but the competition increases every day. In 2011, Aroldis Chapman threw a pitch that measured at 106 mph (170.6 kph) on the scoreboard, 105 mph (169 kph) on a TV broadcast, and 102.4 mph (164.8 kph) on another radar. No one knows which one was correct.

Unfortunately, Chapman was injured in a spring training game in 2014 when a ball struck him in the face, breaking multiple bones. Doctors implanted a titanium plate above his left eye. It took several months, but finally that summer, Chapman was back out on the field and throwing 99 mph (159.3 kph) fastballs once again.

GO DEEPER!

The Magnus effect was described for the first time in 1853 by a German teacher and physicist named Heinrich Gustav Magnus. Along with explaining the movement of spinning balls, the Magnus effect also plays a part in how paintballs fly through the air. Find out how and what this force means next time you suit up for a game of paintball!

Good News—and Bad

The good news is that more and more pitchers are finding ways to throw faster and faster pitches. This makes games more exciting and fun to watch.

The bad news is that these fastballs are causing a lot of injuries to the pitchers.

Pitchers have faced injuries since baseball began. Whenever a pitcher throws a fastball, he is putting even more stress and strain on his shoulder joint. But not all injuries happen during games: in 1994, pitcher Steve Sparks hurt his shoulder while trying to rip a phone

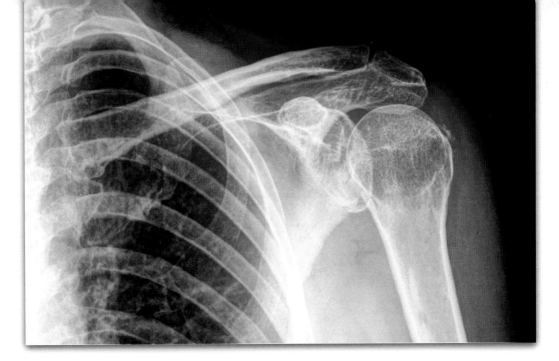

Pitchers are at high risk for shoulder injuries.

book in half. Too much stress threatens not only the ability to pitch but also the ability to use the arm at all!

One of the main reasons a fastball is so physically demanding is the **torque**, or rotation, that is required to throw a ball 100 mph (161 kph). During a pitch, the pitcher's arm snaps forward to release the ball, requiring amazing shoulder rotation. This puts a great deal of strain on the **rotator cuff**. That's the muscles and **tendons** that surround the shoulder joint, keeping the upper bone in your arm within the shoulder **socket**. The intense,

Arm injuries forced the pitcher Tony Saunders to retire at age 26.

[21ST CENTURY SKILLS LIBRARY]

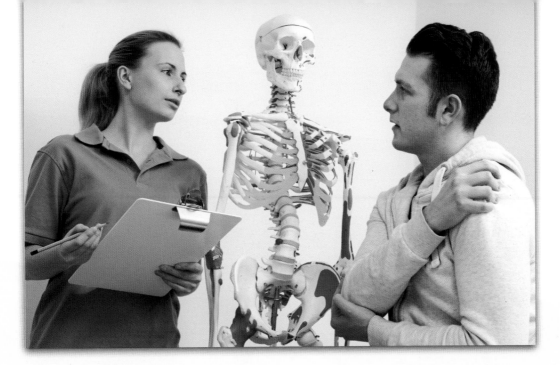

Sports medicine doctors can help treat injured players.

repetitive "whipping" motion that the shoulder makes for each pitch contributes to the muscles' wear and tear.

Finally, once the ball has been released, the **ligaments** and tendons of the arm have to stop moving very quickly, straining them further. Pitchers need to learn the safe way to **decelerate** their arms, in what is commonly known as the follow-through phase.

Some pitchers end up needing physical therapy and even surgery for their shoulder and arm problems. One of the most common operations is known as Tommy John surgery. It is named after the first baseball player

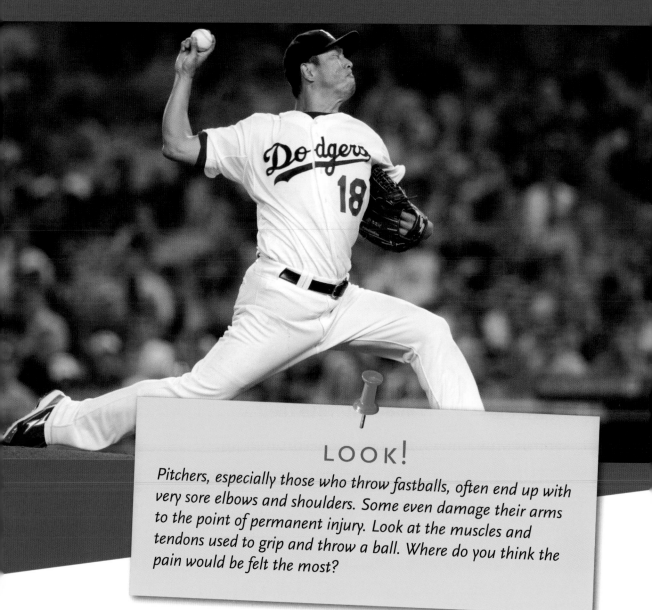

Hiroki Kuroda had to take some time off in 2009 for a sore shoulder.

LOOK!

Pitchers, especially those who throw fastballs, often end up with very sore elbows and shoulders. Some even damage their arms to the point of permanent injury. Look at the muscles and tendons used to grip and throw a ball. Where do you think the pain would be felt the most?

[21ST CENTURY SKILLS LIBRARY]

to have the operation in 1974. In this procedure, a healthy tendon from the arm or leg is used to replace the a damaged elbow ligament.

While the top-notch pitchers from the major league teams risk injuring their arms, so do young players just starting out in Little League or on school teams. For a young pitcher, the rule of thumb is to limit the amount of pitches to his or her age times six (for example, a ten-year-old should be taken out of the game after throwing sixty pitches). Also, he or she shouldn't pitch more than two games per week. By getting enough rest, pitchers can protect their shoulders.

"Throwing Like a Girl"

Imagine having your picture on the cover of one of the biggest sports magazines in the world! The article inside is a feature story about you.

In summer 2014, *Sports Illustrated's* cover featured one person: 13-year-old Mo'ne Davis. She was the first Little League player, male or female, to ever make the cover. At 5 feet 4 inches (162.5 centimeters) and 111 pounds (50 kg), this young woman caught the attention of baseball lovers all across the country. A pitcher for Philadelphia's Taney Dragons, she has already done amazing things on the baseball diamond. She became the first girl in Little League World Series history to throw a **shutout**. She pitched a two-hitter while striking out eight batters.

One of Mo'ne's strengths is her fastball. She has been clocked at 70 mph (112.6 kph), an amazing speed for such a young player. Boys in her age group are commonly throwing fastballs between 50 and 60 mph

Mo'ne Davis performed very well in the 2014 Little League World Series.

Most professional baseball players started out playing on local travel teams at an early age.

(80.4 and 96.5 kph). "Throwing 70 miles an hour—that's throwing like a girl," she said in an interview with CBS.

In addition to being an amazing baseball pitcher, Mo'ne is an honor roll student and a skilled basketball player. In fact, in spite of her performance on the baseball field, her dream is to play for the Women's National Basketball Association. She is on her way to achieving it, too. In December 2014, although she was only in eighth grade, she was placed on her future high school's girls' varsity basketball team as a starter.

THINK ABOUT IT!

The math of a fastball is astounding. At 95 mph (152.8 kph), a baseball travels from the pitcher's mound to the batter in only four-tenths of a second. Batters have thousandths of a second to decide what kind of pitch it is and how to respond. This eye-brain-body coordination is an incredible skill.

*Baseball is one of the most popular
sports in North and South America.*

The fastball is difficult to throw and even harder to
hit. But it is one of the main reasons people around the
world keep coming back to bleacher seats or turning on
their televisions to watch baseball. Many of these fans
never think about air pressure, torque, or rotator cuff
injuries. They just watch the game and cheer when a
fastball hits the triple-digit mark. If they knew what
went into creating that fastball, and the risks pitchers
take whenever they throw one, fans might enjoy—and
respect—that pitch even more.

TIMELINE

A TIMELINE HISTORY OF BASEBALL

ca. 1845	Baseball is officially invented in the United States.
1866	The first women's baseball team is formed.
1884	Baseball rules change to allow overhand throws and fastballs.
1903	Boston plays Pittsburgh in the first World Series.
1921	A baseball game is broadcast on the radio for the first time.
1936	The Baseball Hall of Fame inducts its first players.
1943	The first All-American girls' team is formed.
1946	Bob Feller set a fastball world record at 107.6 mph.
1947	The World Series is first televised.
1974	Nolan Ryan sets a fastball world record for 108.1 mph.
1994	The World Series is canceled because of a baseball strike.
2014	Mo'ne Davis becomes the first girl to throw a shutout in the Little League World Series.

THINK ABOUT IT

Why are tired muscles often at increased risk for injury?
What can a pitcher do to help prevent an arm injury?

How might Mo'ne Davis change baseball for women in
the coming years? Look online for other examples of
girls who compete on teams made up mostly of boys.

What seems more important, the speed of the pitch or
the location of the pitch? If you want to learn more
in-depth about baseball statistics, go online to look up
PITCHf/x, a system that all major league stadiums have
used to track every pitch thrown since 2006. What kinds
of patterns do you notice?

What things can a pitcher do to increase the speed of
his or her fastball? Reread chapters 1 and 3. If a pitcher
were struggling with his or her fastball, what kind of
advice would you give?

LEARN MORE

FURTHER READING

Barr, George. *Sports Science for Young People*. New York: Dover Publications, 2011.

Bonnet, Robert, and Dan Keen. *Home Run! Science Projects with Baseball and Softball*. Berkeley Heights, NJ: Enslow Publishers, 2009.

Dreier, David L. *Baseball: How It Works*. Mankato, MN: Capstone Press, 2010.

Hantula, Richard. *Science at Work in Baseball*. New York: Marshall Cavendish, 2012.

WEB SITES

Brooks Baseball—Pitch Tracking. Simplified.
http://www.brooksbaseball.net/
Look around this site for tons of baseball data.

NBC News—The Math and Science of Baseball
http://www.nbcnews.com/id/39446333/ns/technology_and_science-science/t/
math-science-baseball/#.VSXPLYctH4g
Find out some surprising answers to tricky questions about baseball.

PBS—Science of Sports: Better Baseball
www.pbs.org/safarchive/4_class/45_pguides/pguide_405/4545_bb.html
Try some basic physics experiments to help you understand pitching better.

Student Science—Baseball: From Pitch to Hits
https://student.societyforscience.org/article/baseball-pitch-hits
Read about Detroit Tigers pitcher Jose Valverde and the specific pitches he used in a 2013 game against the Kansas City Royals.

GLOSSARY

aerodynamics (air-oh-dye-NAM-iks) the branch of mechanics that deals with the motion of air and the effects of motion

amateurs (AM-uh-churz) unpaid baseball players

boundary layer (BOUN-dree LAY-ur) the pocket of air that forms around a fastball

catcher (KETCH-ur) the player who squats behind home plate and signals to the pitcher which pitches to throw, and catches pitches that aren't hit

decelerate (di-SEL-uh-rate) to reduce speed or slow down

ligaments (LIG-uh-muhnts) tough pieces of tissue in the body that hold bones together and keep organs in place

pelvis (PEL-vis) the wide, curved bones between the spine and the leg bones

pitcher (PICH-ur) the player who throws the ball to the batter in baseball

rotator cuff (ROH-tay-tur KUF) the group of muscles and tendons around the shoulder

shutout (SHUT-out) a game in which one side does not score

socket (SOK-it) a hollow part in a bone that holds another bone

statisticians (stah-tuhs-TISH-uhnz) people who collect and study statistics and numbers

tendons (TEN-duhnz) tough pieces of tissue in the body connecting muscle to bone

torque (TORK) a force that causes something to rotate

INDEX